Why is the Sky Blue?

and other outdoor questions

by Catherine Ripley

illustrated by Scot Ritchie

OXFORD UNIVERSITY PRESS

Oxford University Press, Great Clarendon Street, Oxford OX2 6DP

Oxford New York
Athens Aukland Bangkok Bogotá Bombay
Buenos Aires Calcutta Cape Town Dar es Salaam
Delhi Florence Hong Kong Istanbul Karachi
Kuala Lumpur Madras Madrid Melbourne
Mexico City Nairobi Paris Singapore
Taipei Tokyo Toronto Warsaw

and associated companies in
Berlin Ibadan

Oxford is a trade mark of Oxford University Press

Text © 1997 Catherine Ripley
Illustrations © 1997 Scot Ritchie

First published by Owl Books,
PO Box 53, 370 King Street West, Ste. 300
Toronto, ON, Canada
M5V 1J9

This edition published by
Oxford University Press 1997
1 3 5 7 9 10 8 6 4 2

DEDICATION

For faithful dogs everywhere — especially Rip, Chimney Sweep, Cinders, Tarfoot, Tucker, Kelsey, Duff, Nikki, and even though I don't know him personally, Scot's dog...Ollie!

A CIP catalogue record for this book is available from the British Library.

ISBN 0-19-910457-3 (hardback)
ISBN 0-19-910458-1 (paperback)

Printed in Hong Kong

Contents

Why does it smell so fresh after it rains?

Because the air is clean and wet. First the rain washes floating bits, like dust and soot, out of the air. Then the wetness keeps the bits down on the ground, so they don't get in the way of you sniffing other stuff. Wet air carries the smells of the wet trees, grass and earth to your nose better than dry air does. The moisture in the air even makes the inside of your nose wetter, the better to trap all those fresh smells!

Why do worms come out when it's wet?

Because worms like it wet! They always need to stay a little wet or their skin will dry out. When it is sunny, they stay underground in the moist soil. But when it rains, they don't have to worry about the sun drying them up. Out of the ground they squirm to hunt for food. Sometimes it rains after a long dry spell, and all kinds of new plants and animals start to grow underground. They use up a lot of the air that worms need to breathe. Then the worms have to tunnel up and go out above the ground to breathe.

Why do dogs sniff everything?

Sniff-sniff-sniffing is a dog's way of checking things out. A dog's nose can smell things about 40 times better than your nose can. By sniffing, a dog can tell who has been around its home area recently. It can tell if there is another dog nearby. It can tell if the animals it meets (and that includes you) are afraid or happy. A dog also sniffs to find food or to hunt down an interesting-smelling animal, such as a rabbit or — *meow* — a cat!

Ow! How does my cut stop bleeding?

It's a sticky story. As soon as you cut yourself, parts of your blood called platelets start to gather. They stick to each other and to the edges of your cut, forming a thin cover over it. If the cut is big, the platelets may need extra help to stop the bleeding. Along comes fibrin to the rescue. Fibrin is another special part of your blood. It weaves a criss-crossing tangle of long, sticky strands over the cut. Then the strands dry out to make a scab. The scab acts like a bandage, and lets new skin grow underneath. So whatever you do, don't pick at it!

Why do dandelions turn white and fluffy?

So they can make more dandelions! Every dandelion bloom is made up of more than a hundred tiny yellow flowers. A seed forms inside each flower, and gets attached to a long stalk. At the top of the stalks are white tufts. When the yellow petals fall off, all you see is a white ball of fluff. The fluffy tufts are like little kites, each carrying a seed. Along comes the wind, and carries the tufts and their seeds far and wide. The seeds get spread all around, and every seed could grow into a new dandelion.

Why is the sky blue?

Because of scattered blue light waves. Believe it or not, clear light is made up of all the colours in the rainbow — red, orange, yellow, green, blue, indigo and violet. These colours travel in waves. When light hits things, some of the colour waves are soaked up, and others bounce off. Whatever waves bounce back to your eyes, those are the colours you see!

High in the sky, the waves of light from the sun hit the air. Air is made up of different gases in tiny, tiny bits called molecules. The blue light waves bounce off these bits of air, and scatter all over the sky. So when you look up, it's blue as far as you can see.

What's that white line in the sky?

It's a trail of ice! It shows you where a jet plane has been. Jet planes have engines to make them move. As the engines work, they let off exhaust that includes water so hot it's like steam coming out of a kettle. When the hot exhaust hits the air outside the plane, the steam cools and turns into water droplets. A second later, the water droplets turn into ice in the fre-e-e-e-zing cold air way up high. These little pieces of ice make a long, white trail behind the plane as it moves.

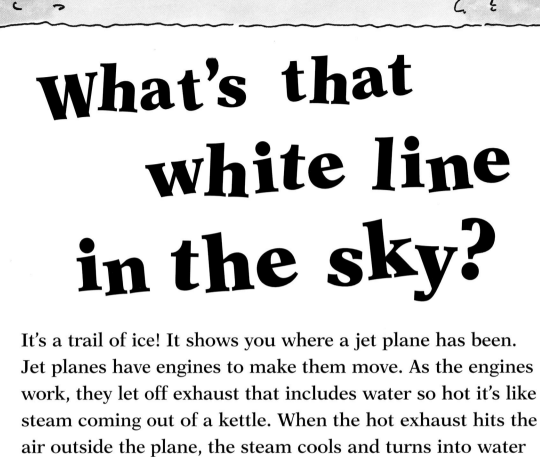

Why do I feel funny inside when I swing?

Because you're out of balance. It all starts deep in your ears. Messages go from here to your brain. They tell your brain which way you're going and how fast you're going. That's how you keep your balance. When you swing, your body changes its place so fast, the messages can't keep up. Your brain gets a little confused. And when your brain is a little confused, you might feel mixed up inside. The same thing can happen on a roller coaster or even in a lift — whee!

Why do some rocks sparkle?

Because parts of the rock are as smooth as a mirror. Even if a rock looks rough, some of its very small parts can be smooth and flat. When light hits something smooth, some of it bounces off. Just think of how light shines off a mirror. And the more smooth parts the light has to bounce off, the more sparkles it makes. So rocks with lots of little smooth parts really sparkle and shine.

Why do birds sing?

They're talking! If birds sang in words, you'd hear
a lot of different messages. In springtime you might
hear a male bird's song that says both "Stay away"
and "Come and be my sweetie". To other male birds,
it's a message to keep out of the singing bird's area,
but female birds hear the same call as an invitation
to come right in! Birds sing out all kinds of messages.
Baby birds call "I'm hun-hun-hungry, Mum and Dad!"
Birds in a flock will call to stay together, singing "I'm
here, but where are you?" Some birds will even warn
each other of danger, calling "Watch out, watch out
wherever you are!" All in bird talk, of course.

What's a shadow?

It's where light isn't. Light can't travel through things that get in its way. For example, when sunlight hits you, it's stopped by your body, while all around you it reaches the ground. Where you block light from reaching the ground, a dark shape is formed . . . your shadow! It goes with you everywhere — see for yourself on a sunny day.

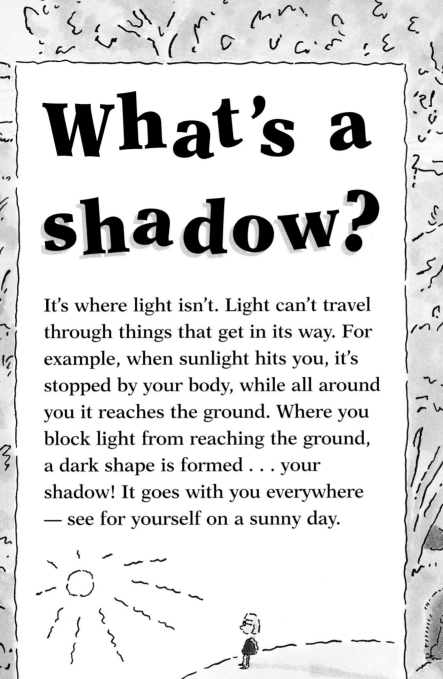

Where do puddles go?

Up, down, and all around. Sometimes a thirsty animal will lap up some of the puddle water, so the puddle gets smaller. Much of the water seeps down out of sight into the soil. When it stops raining, what's left of a puddle starts to dry up. The water floats away into the air all around, like water from wet clothes hanging up to dry. Going, going, gone!

Outdoor Eit.

Some clouds look like giant cotton balls. Just right for jumping into? Not really! Jumping into a cloud would be like jumping into fog — cold, damp, and clammy. Clouds are made of millions and millions of tiny drops of cold water, and sometimes tiny ice crystals, too.

It's raining . . . hamburgers? Raindrops are nice and round way up high in the clouds. But as they fall to Earth, the air pushing against them flattens them into mini-hamburger-shaped drops!

Have you ever noticed that dogs pee a little in a lot of places? Like their relatives, the wolves, dogs do this to mark out an area as their home. When other dogs sniff these spots, they know they have to behave in this dog's home area, get out, or fight to stay and be top dog.